# THE
# PROJECT CYCLE

**WARREN C. BAUM**

*Library of Congress Cataloging in Publication Data*

Baum, Warren C.
  The project cycle.

  1. World Bank.   2. Economic development projects
I. Title.
HG3881.B365   1982      332.1'532      82-8468
ISBN 0-8213-0022-9                     AACR2

This pamphlet is based on an article by Warren C. Baum, Vice President, Operations Policy, that originally appeared in the December 1978 issue of *Finance & Development*. It was prepared with the assistance of Herman G. van der Tak and John A. King.

# THE PROJECT CYCLE

If the question, "What does the World Bank do?" had to be answered in a few words, those words would be: "It lends for development projects." The Bank's main business is to lend for specific projects, carefully selected and prepared, thoroughly appraised, closely supervised, and systematically evaluated. Since opening its doors in 1946, the Bank—in the context of this pamphlet, the International Bank for Reconstruction and Development and its soft-loan affiliate, the International Development Association (IDA), which began operations in 1961—has made some 3,094 development loans and credits for a total of more than $92 billion. Of these, the overwhelming majority, over 90 percent, have been for specific projects such as schools, crop production programs, hydroelectric power dams, roads, and fertilizer plants.

This concentration on project lending is directed at ensuring that Bank funds are invested in sound, productive projects that contribute to the development of a borrowing country's economy as well as to its capacity to repay the loan. The Bank is both a developmental and a financial institution, and each project for which it lends must satisfy both features of the institution.

The numbers of projects and the amounts loaned have grown markedly over recent years. In the early 1950s, the Bank was making fewer than twenty loans a year, mostly in Europe and Latin America, totaling about $400 million. In fiscal year 1967, there were sixty-seven loans, more widely spread geographically, totaling $1.1 billion. In the fiscal year ending in June 1981, 246 loans, totaling $12.3 billion, were approved for ninety countries.

There has been no less a change in the character of projects. Bank lending has become increasingly development oriented in terms of borrowing countries, development strategy, sectors of lending, and project design.

— In terms of *countries:* Lending has been directed increasingly toward the poor and less developed countries in Asia, Africa, and Latin America.

— In terms of *development strategy:* The so-called trickle-down theory, which assumes that the benefits of growth will

3

eventually reach the masses of the poor, has been replaced in the Bank by a more balanced approach, combining accelerated growth with a direct attack on poverty through programs to raise the productivity and living standards of the rural and urban poor.

— In terms of *sectors:* The emphasis has shifted from basic infrastructure (roads, railways, power) and industry to more comprehensive programs aimed at growth, provision of basic services, and improvment of income distribution. While infrastructure continues to be important, lending for agriculture and rural development, oil and gas, urban sites and services, water supply and sanitation, small-scale enterprises, education, health, population, and nutrition has been introduced or greatly expanded.

— In terms of *project design:* Greater attention is given in all sectors, both new and traditional, to income distribution and employment, development of local resources and institutions, training of local personnel, impact on environment, and overcoming social and cultural constraints. The Bank has not diminished, however, the attention that it has always paid to market forces, realistic pricing, good management, and the recovery, where feasible, of project costs to permit adequate maintenance and replication.

This evolution in the development orientation—and in the quality—of Bank lending can be illustrated, at the risk of oversimplification, by comparing a "typical" loan of the 1950s with a "typical" loan of the 1970s.

The 1950s loan might be for power generation in a middle-income developing country. In a sense it would be an "enclave" project, designed and supervised by foreign consultants, executed by foreign contractors and suppliers, and managed with the help of expatriates. The technical and financial viability of the project would be analyzed, as would its organization and management, but little attention would be paid to its setting within the energy sector, to how the electricity would be distributed, and to the impact of the level and structure of tariffs on power consumption.

The loan of the 1970s would be for rural development in a low-income developing country. It would provide an integrated package of goods and services (extension, credit, marketing, storage, infrastructure, research) to raise the productivity and living standards of farmers. Existing local institutions would be strengthened or new ones established;

4

local staff would be used as much as possible, with the help of extensive training programs; low-cost design and appropriate technology would be emphasized, giving greater opportunities for local contractors and sources of supply; a system of monitoring and evaluation would be built in to help adjust the project as it went forward and to draw lessons for future projects; and attention would be paid to cost recovery from beneficiaries so that the project would be replicable.

Notwithstanding this record of growth and change, the Bank is still dealing with a relatively small number of quite large projects; the average loan is now about $50 million for a total project investment of $140 million. Bank-assisted projects can have an important demonstration effect and can encourage other investors to supplement Bank lending with their own, as cofinancers or separately; approximately one-third of Bank assisted projects in 1981 had cofinancing from foreign sources.

Every Bank-assisted project must contribute substantially to development objectives and be economically, technically, and financially sound. No two projects are alike; each has its own history, and lending has to be tailored to its circumstances. On the other hand, each project passes through a cycle that, with some variations, is common to all. This pamphlet will discuss the phases of the project cycle—identification, preparation, appraisal, negotiation and presentation to the Executive Directors, implementation and supervision, and evaluation—and the Bank's role in each of them. Each phase leads to the next, and the last phases, in turn, produce new project approaches and ideas and lead to the identification of new projects, making the cycle self-renewing.

The Bank's role in the project cycle is performed largely by its projects staff, who now number about 1,300 drawn from 100 nationalities. Projects staff comprise almost three-quarters of all operational staff employed by the Bank and nearly half of all professional staff. Though there are substantial groups of economists, financial analysts, and various kinds of engineers, an extraordinary variety of other disciplines is also represented: agronomists, specialists in tropical agriculture, groundwater, agricultural credit or livestock, demographers, architects, rural and urban sociologists, public health experts, environmentalists, educators, energy specialists, and physical planners. Typically, technical specialists come to the Bank in mid-career, after extensive experience in their field, sometimes as managers. Most have worked in developing countries. Projects staff are expected to have a broad

5

understanding of development issues and the capacity and maturity to make sound, independent judgments. It is safe to say that, in terms of size and national and professional diversity, the Bank's projects staff is unique.

## IDENTIFICATION

The first phase of the cycle is concerned with identifying projects that have a high priority, that appear suitable for Bank support, and that the Bank, the government, and the borrower are interested in considering (see box for the definition of a borrower). In earlier years, project identification was done *ad hoc,* largely in response to proposals by governments and borrowers. Over the years, the Bank has encouraged and helped borrowing countries to develop their own planning capabilities and has also strengthened its own methods of project generation. Economic and sector analyses carried out by the Bank provide a framework for evaluating national and sectoral policies and problems and an understanding of the development potential of the country. They also assess a country's "creditworthiness" for Bank or IDA lending. This analysis

6

provides the basis for a continuing dialogue between the Bank and a country on an appropriate development strategy, including policy and institutional changes for the economy as a whole and for its major sectors. It is then possible to identify projects that fit into and support a coherent development strategy, that meet sectoral objectives, and that both the government and the Bank consider suitable. These projects must also meet a *prima facie* test of feasibility—that technical and institutional solutions are likely to be found at costs commensurate with expected benefits.

Identifying a project that meets these requirements is not easy. Knowledge required for reaching sound judgments may be lacking. The government and other lending agencies may not share the Bank's views on development objectives or sector priorities. There may be difficult choices regarding the scope of the project (Should it start with a pilot/experimental phase or with a larger but possibly more risky investment?). Differences may quickly surface over the need for policy or institutional reforms to achieve the project's objectives. Work on resolving some of these issues may extend well into the preparation stage.

In practice, how are projects identified within this context? Both the Bank and the government are involved, making the process complex, and this complexity is compounded by the differing capabilities of governments for handling economic planning and project generation. The Bank's economic analysis of a country is affected by the extent and quality of the country's data base and its own economic work. Sector analysis might be done by the country itself, or might be carried out by the Bank or through one of the Bank's cooperative programs with a specialized UN agency, or through studies financed by the United Nations Development Programme (UNDP), bilateral aid programs, or a specific provision for studies in a previous Bank loan.

Finally, some projects are brought forward by private sponsors, such as mining and petroleum enterprises, seeking to develop new resources. These projects have to meet the standards described previously before being regarded as "identified" from the Bank's point of view.

Once identified, projects are incorporated into a multi-year lending program for each country that forms the basis for the Bank's future work in the country. Country programs are used for programming and budgeting the Bank's operations and for assuring that the resources necessary to bring each project forward through the successive phases of its cycle are available.

7

# PREPARATION

After a project has been incorporated into the lending program, it enters the project pipeline, and an extensive period—normally one or two years—of close collaboration between the Bank and the eventual borrower begins. A "project brief" is prepared for each project, describing its objectives, identifying principal issues, and establishing the timetable for its further processing. It is difficult to generalize about the preparation phase because of the variables that abound: the nature of the project, the experience and capability of the borrower, the knowledge currently available (Is it the first loan to the sector/borrower or a "repeater"?), the sources and availability of financing for preparation, and the nature of the relationships between the Bank, the government, cofinancers, and other donors that may be involved in the sector or project.

Formal responsibility for preparation rests with the borrower. At one time, the Bank was reluctant to assist in project preparation, on the banker's principle that such involvement might prejudice its objectivity at appraisal. But experience has shown that the Bank must have an active role in ensuring a timely flow of well-prepared projects. That role has a number of aspects: making sure that borrowers with the capacity and resources to prepare projects themselves understand the Bank's requirements and standards; helping other borrowers to find the financing or technical assistance necessary for preparatory work; and filling gaps in projects that have been incompletely or inadequately prepared. There are even exceptional circumstances in which the Bank itself does preparatory work. The Bank's regional missions in Eastern and Western Africa were established primarily to supplement the limited capabilities of governments in those regions to identify and prepare sound projects.

Financial and technical assistance for project preparation can be extended in a number of ways. The Bank can provide special loans for technical assistance or detailed engineering, make advances from its Project Preparation Facility, reimburse the borrower under the loan in question for preparatory work done earlier, or include funds for preparatory work in a loan for another project in the sector. Cooperative programs between the Bank and the Food and Agriculture Organization of the United Nations (FAO), the United Nations Educational, Scientific, and Cultural Organization (Unesco), the World Health Organization (WHO), and the United Nations Industrial Development Organization (UNIDO) are also an important source of support, as are the UNDP and bilateral aid programs.

While most other assistance for project preparation is provided on a grant basis, and hence is especially attractive, Bank financing must be repaid by the borrower. In providing this help, care must be taken that the project is not perceived at this stage as "the Bank's project" and that the government and the borrower are fully committed to the project and deeply involved in its preparation. This care is more relevant to the "new-style" projects than to traditional infrastructure projects that involve well-established entities whose objectives, and ways of achieving them, are reasonably clear. In new-style projects, such conditions often do not exist, so the commitment of the government and the borrower is essential not only for preparation, but, even more, for successful implementation.

Preparation must cover the full range of technical, institutional, economic, and financial conditions necessary to achieve the project's objectives. For example, a resettlement project might require studies based on remote sensing data to locate arable land, transportation corridors, and the population living in the area proposed for resettlement. Verification on the ground would be followed by a more detailed investigation of soils and water resources; determination of appropriate cropping patterns on the basis of available resources and research knowledge; selection of

9

the technical package necessary for increasing crop yields; and economic and sociological studies of the people being settled to determine appropriate systems of land tenure, extension services, marketing systems, project management, and other institutional arrangements. Government policies with respect to the costs of inputs and the prices of farm products would be studied, as well as levels and methods of cost recovery and their impact on the financial position of the beneficiaries and the government. The role of the private sector in relation to the project would be yet another subject to be examined.

A critical element of preparation is identifying and comparing technical and institutional alternatives for achieving the project's objectives. Most developing countries are characterized by abundant, inexpensive labor and scarce capital. The Bank, therefore, is not looking for the most advanced technological solutions, but for those that are most appropriate to the country's resource endowment and stage of development. Though the Bank has financed advanced telecommunications equipment and modern container-port facilities, project officers nevertheless must consider such questions as whether oxen are more economical than tractors for crop cultivation; whether slum upgrading or sites and services are more suitable than conventional housing as minimal accommodation for the urban poor; or whether public standpipes are more appropriate than house connections for water supply. Preparation thus requires feasibility studies that identify and prepare preliminary designs of technical and institutional alternatives, compare their respective costs and benefits, and investigate in more detail the more promising alternatives until the most satisfactory solution is finally worked out.

All this takes time, and the Bank is sometimes criticized for the length of time required to make a loan. But for the countries concerned, each project represents a major investment with a long economic life, and the time spent in arriving at the best technical solution, in setting up the proper organization, and in anticipating and dealing in advance with marketing and other problems, usually pays for itself several times over.

# APPRAISAL

As the project takes shape and studies near completion, the project is scheduled for appraisal. Appraisal, perhaps the best known phase of project work (in part, because it is the culmination of preparatory work), provides a comprehensive review of all aspects of the project and lays the foundation for implementing the project and evaluating it when completed.

Appraisal is solely the Bank's responsibility. It is conducted by Bank staff, sometimes supplemented by individual consultants, who usually spend three to four weeks in the field. If preparation has been done well, appraisal can be relatively straightforward; if not, a subsequent mission, or missions, to the country may be necessary to complete the job. Appraisal covers four major aspects of the project—technical, institutional, economic, and financial.

TECHNICAL. The Bank has to ensure that projects are soundly designed, appropriately engineered, and follow accepted agronomic, educational, or other standards. The appraisal mission looks into technical alternatives considered, solutions proposed, and expected results.

More concretely, technical appraisal is concerned with questions of physical scale, layout, and location of facilities; what technology is to be used, including types of equipment or processes and their appropriateness to local conditions; what approach will be followed for the provision of services; how realistic implementation schedules are; and what the likelihood is of achieving expected levels of output. In a family planning project, the technical appraisal might be concerned with the number, design, and location of maternal and child health clinics and the appropriateness of the services offered to the needs of the population being served; in highways, with the width and pavement of the roads in relation to expected traffic and the trade-offs between initial construction costs and recurrent costs for maintenance, and between more or less labor-intensive methods of construction; in education, with whether the proposed curriculum and the number and layout of classrooms, laboratories, and other facilities are suited to the country's educational needs.

A critical part of technical appraisal is a review of the cost estimates and the engineering or other data on which they are based to determine whether they are accurate within an acceptable margin and whether allowances for physical contingencies and expected price increases during implementation are adequate. The technical appraisal also reviews proposed procurement arrangements to make sure that the Bank's requirements are met. Procedures for obtaining engineering, architectural, or other professional services are examined. In addition, technical appraisal is concerned with estimating the costs of operating project facilities and services and with the availability of necessary raw materials or other inputs. The potential impact of the project on the human and physical environment is examined to make sure that any adverse effects will be controlled or minimized.

INSTITUTIONAL. In the Bank's current terminology, "institution building" has become perhaps the most important purpose of Bank lending. This means that the transfer of financial resources and the construction of physical facilities, however valuable in their own right, are less important in the long run than the creation of a sound and viable local "institution," interpreted in its broadest sense to cover not only the borrowing entity itself, its organization, management, staffing, policies, and procedures, but also the whole array of government policies that conditions the environment in which the institution operates.

Experience indicates that insufficient attention to the institutional aspects of a project leads to problems during its

12

implementation and operation. Institutional appraisal is concerned with a host of questions, such as whether the entity is properly organized and its management adequate to do the job, whether local capabilities and initiative are being used effectively, and whether policy or institutional changes are required outside the entity to achieve project objectives.

These questions are important for traditional project entities; they are even more important (and difficult to answer) for the entities charged with preparing and carrying out the new-style projects intended to benefit the rural and urban poor, where there may be no established institutional pattern to follow. The Bank's experience to date has not yielded any ready-made solutions for putting together an institution that can effectively and economically deliver goods and services to large numbers of people—often in remote areas and outside the ordinary ambit of government—and that can motivate them and change their behavior.

Of all the aspects of a project, institution building is perhaps the most difficult to come to grips with. In part, this is because its success depends so much on an understanding of the cultural environment. The Bank has come to recognize the need for a continuing re-examination of institutional arrangements, an openness to new ideas, and a willingness to adopt a long-term approach that may extend over several projects.

ECONOMIC. Through cost-benefit analysis of alternative project designs, the one that contributes most to the development objectives of the country may be selected. This analysis is normally done in successive stages during project preparation, but appraisal is the point at which the final review and assessment are made.

During economic appraisal, the project is studied in its sectoral setting. The investment program for the sector, the strengths and weaknesses of public and private sectoral institutions, and key government policies are all examined.

In transportation, each appraisal considers the transportation system as a whole and its contribution to the country's economic development. A highway appraisal examines the relationship with competing modes of transport such as railways. Transport policies throughout the sector are reviewed and changes recommended, for example, in any regulatory practices that distort the allocation of traffic. In education, power, and telecommunications, the "project" as defined by the Bank may embrace the investment program of

13

the whole sector. In agriculture, which is more diversified and accounts for a much larger share of a developing country's economic activity, it is more difficult to formulate a comprehensive strategy for the sector; attention is given to sectoral issues such as land tenure, the adequacy of incentives for farmers, marketing arrangements, availability of public services, and governmental tax, pricing, and subsidy policies.

Whenever the current state of the art permits, projects are subjected to a detailed analysis of their costs and benefits to the country, the result of which is usually expressed as an economic rate of return. This analysis often requires the solution of difficult problems, such as how to determine the physical consequences of the project and how to value them in terms of the development objectives of the country.

Over the years, the Bank has kept in close touch with progress in the methodology of economic appraisal. "Shadow" prices are used routinely when true economic values of costs are not reflected in market prices as a result of various distortions, such as trade restrictions, taxes, or subsidies. These shadow price adjustments are made most frequently in the exchange rate and labor costs used in the calculations. The distribution of the benefits of a project and its fiscal impact are considered carefully, and the use of "social" prices to give proper weight in the cost-benefit analysis to the government's objectives of improved income distribution and increased public savings is passing through an experimental phase. Since the estimates of future costs and benefits are subject to substantial margins of error, an analysis is always made of the sensitivity of the return on the project to variations in some of the key assumptions.

Less frequently, in cases of major uncertainty, a risk/probability analysis is also carried out. The optimal timing of the investment is tested in relation to the first year's benefits. When the Bank provides funds to intermediate agencies (development finance companies, agricultural credit institutions) for relending to smaller operations, or in the case of sector lending, those agencies' own appraisal methods must be acceptable.

Some of the elements of project costs and benefits, such as pollution control, better health or education, or manpower training, may defy quantification; in other projects, for example electric power or telecommunications, it may be necessary to use proxies, such as revenues, that do not fully measure the value of the service to the economy. In some cases, it is possible to assess alternative solutions that have the same benefits and to select the least-cost solution. In other cases, for example education, alternatives are likely to involve different benefits as well as different costs, and a qualitative assessment must suffice. Whether qualitative or quantitative, the economic analysis always aims at assessing the contribution of the project to the development objectives of the country; this remains the basic criterion for project selection and appraisal. And while greater concern with the distributional effects of projects reflects broader objectives of development, it does not mean that the Bank has lowered its standards of appraisal. Whether "old" style or "new," every project must have a satisfactory economic return, a standard that the Bank believes serves the best interests of both the country and the Bank itself.

FINANCIAL. Financial appraisal has several purposes. One is to ensure that there are sufficient funds to cover the costs of implementing the project. The Bank does not normally lend for all project costs; typically, it finances foreign exchange costs and expects the borrower or the government to meet some or all of the local costs. In addition, other cofinancers, such as the European Development Fund, the several Arab funds, the regional development banks, bilateral aid agencies, and a growing number of commercial banks, are joining to an increasing extent in cofinancing projects that, in many instances, are appraised and supervised by the Bank. Therefore, an important aspect of appraisal is to ensure that there is a financing plan that will make funds available to implement the project on schedule. When funds are to be provided by a government known to have difficulty in raising local revenues, special arrangements may be proposed, such as advance appropriations to a revolving fund or the earmarking of tax proceeds.

For a revenue-producing enterprise, financial appraisal is also concerned with financial viability. Will it be able to meet all its financial obligations, including debt service to the Bank? Will it be able to generate enough funds from internal resources to earn a reasonable rate of return on its assets and make a satisfactory contribution to its future capital requirements? The finances of the enterprise are closely reviewed through projections of the balance sheet, income statement, and cash flow. Where financial accounts are inadequate, a new accounting system may be established with technical assistance financed out of the loan. Additional safeguards of financial integrity may include establishing suitable debt-to-equity ratios or limitations on additional long-term borrowing.

The financial review often highlights the need to adjust the level and structure of prices charged by the enterprise. Whether or not they are publicly owned, enterprises assisted by the Bank generally provide basic services and come under close public scrutiny. Because the government may wish to subsidize such services to the consuming public as a matter of policy, or perhaps simply as the line of least resistance, it may be reluctant to approve the price increases necessary to ensure efficient use of the output of the enterprise and to meet its financial objectives. But adequate prices are a *sine qua non* of Bank lending to revenue-earning enterprises, and the question of rate adjustments may be critical to the appraisal and subsequent implementation of a project.

Financial appraisal is also concerned with recovering investment and operating costs from project beneficiaries. The Bank normally expects farmers to pay, over time and out of their increased production, all of the operating costs and at least a substantial part of the capital costs of, say, an irrigation project. Actual recovery in each case takes account of the income position of the beneficiaries and of practical problems such as the difficulties of administering a particular system of charges or of levying higher charges on Bank-assisted projects than are collected elsewhere. The Bank's policy thus tries to strike a balance between considerations of equity, the need to use scarce resources efficiently, and the need to generate additional funds to replicate the project and reach larger numbers of potential beneficiaries.

Costs can be recovered in a variety of ways—by charges for irrigation water, through general taxation, or by requiring farmers to sell their crops to a government marketing agency at controlled prices. Some countries apply lower standards of cost recovery than those recommended by the Bank; thus, arriving at a common judgment on what is desirable and practicable can be one of the more difficult aspects of the appraisal and subsequent negotiation.

To ensure the efficient use of scarce capital, the Bank believes that interest charges to the ultimate beneficiaries should generally reflect the opportunity cost of money in the economy (indicating the cost of foregone alternatives). But interest rates are often subsidized, and the rate of inflation may even exceed the interest rate. In countries with high rates of inflation, a system of indexed rates is sometimes followed. As in the case of cost recovery, the appropriate level of interest rates may be a contentious issue. The Bank may have to set its sights on a long-term goal, recognizing that it will take time to bring about what may be far-reaching changes in financial policy. This may be particularly so when the government is seeking to control interest rates and other prices as part of an anti-inflation program.

The appraisal mission prepares a report that sets forth its findings and recommends terms and conditions of the loan. This report is drafted and redrafted and carefully reviewed before the loan is approved by the management of the Bank for negotiations with the borrower. Because of the Bank's close involvement in identification and preparation, appraisal rarely results in rejection of a project; but it may be extensively modified or redesigned during this process to correct flaws that otherwise might have led to its rejection.

# NEGOTIATIONS, BOARD PRESENTATION

Negotiation is the stage at which the Bank and the borrower endeavor to agree on the measures necessary to assure the success of the project. These agreements are then converted into legal obligations, set out in the loan documents. The Bank may have agreed with a public utility borrower that, to earn an adequate rate of return and finance a reasonable proportion of its investments, prices are to be increased by, say, 20 percent immediately and 10 percent in two years' time. A financial covenant to be agreed upon during negotiation will define the overall financial objectives and specify the necessary rate of return and the timing of the initial rate increase. If a new project unit must be set up to administer the project or to coordinate the activities of the various ministries involved, the loan documents will specify when and how it is to be established and staffed. In fact, all of the principal issues that have been raised prior to and during appraisal are dealt with in the loan documents. Thus, the drafting and negotiation of the legal documents are an essential part of the process of ensuring that the borrower and the Bank are in agreement, not only on the broad objectives of the project, but also on the specific actions necessary to achieve them and the detailed schedule for project implementation.

Negotiations are a process of give and take on both sides of the table. The Bank, for its part, must learn to adapt its general policies to what can reasonably be accomplished in the country, the sector, and the particular setting of the project. The borrower, for its part, must recognize that the Bank's advice is generally based on professional expertise and worldwide experience, and that the Bank's requirement that its funds be invested wisely is compatible with the best interests of the project. Despite differences that inevitably arise when difficult issues must be resolved, the relations that have developed over time between the Bank and its borrowers at this and other stages of the project cycle are generally very good. Bank staff have become more aware of, and sensitive to, local conditions that are critical to the success of a project. Borrowers have come to appreciate that the Bank's approach is professional and objective, that it is in business to lend for well-conceived and well-executed projects, and that this is indeed the Bank's only interest in project work.

After negotiations, the appraisal report, amended to reflect the agreements reached, together with the President's report and the loan documents, is presented to the Bank's Executive Directors. If the Executive Directors approve the operation, the loan is then signed in a simple ceremony that marks the end of one stage of the cycle and the beginning of another.

# IMPLEMENTATION AND SUPERVISION

The next stage in the life of a project is its actual implementation over the period of construction and subsequent operation. Implementation, of course, is the responsibility of the borrower, with whatever assistance has been agreed upon with the Bank in such forms as organizational studies, training of staff, expatriate managers, or consultants to help supervise construction. The Bank's role is to supervise the project as it is implemented.

Supervision is the least glamorous part of project work, but in several respects it is the most important. Once the loan for a particular project is signed, attention in the borrowing country shifts to new projects that are coming along; this attitude is understandable and it is reinforced by the fact that many months or years may elapse before the "old" project begins to yield tangible results. Nevertheless, it is obvious that no matter how well a project has been identified, prepared, and appraised, its development benefits can be realized only when it has been properly executed. All projects face implementation problems, some of which cannot be foreseen. These problems may stem from difficulties inherent in the development process or from more specific causes such as changes in the economic and political situation, in project management, or even in the weather. As a result, although the development objectives of a project generally remain constant, its implementation path often varies from that which was envisaged.

It is for these reasons that the Bank has decided that adequate supervision should be the first priority in the assignment of project staff. In practice, the resources devoted to supervision have increased substantially over the years, both absolutely and relative to other project tasks.

The Bank is required by its Articles of Agreement to make arrangements to "ensure that the proceeds of any loan are used only for the purposes for which the loan was granted." While this "watchdog" function has been and remains important, the main purpose of supervision is to help ensure that projects achieve their development objectives and, in particular, to work with the borrowers in identifying and dealing with problems that arise during implementation. Supervision, therefore, is primarily an exercise in collective problem solving, and, as such, is one of the most effective ways in which the Bank provides technical assistance to its member countries.

Over the years another central objective of supervision has emerged: gathering the accumulated experience to "feed back" into the design and preparation of future projects and into the improvement of policies and procedures. Monitoring and evaluation units are now frequently incorporated, particularly in the new-style projects, to gather information for this purpose. An annual review of the supervision portfolio as a whole is conducted to identify major issues of implementation and recommend appropriate changes in Bank policies and procedures.

Supervision takes place in a variety of ways. During negotiation, agreement will have been reached on a schedule of progress reports to be submitted by the borrower. These reports cover the physical execution of the project, its costs, the financial status of revenue-earning enterprises, and information on the evolution of project benefits.

Progress reports are reviewed at headquarters. Problems that surface are dealt with by correspondence or in the course of the field missions that are sent to every project. The frequency of these missions is closely tailored to the complexity of the project, the status of its implementation, and the number and nature of problems encountered. In the periodic internal reviews of projects under supervision, currently numbering about 1,600, some projects are classified as belonging to a special "problem" category. These projects, usually about 10 percent of the total, are watched with particular care and may be visited three or four times a year.

An important element of project supervision concerns procurement of goods and works financed under the loan. Procurement is carried out in accordance with guidelines, incorporated into every loan agreement, that are designed to ensure that the requisite goods and works are procured in the most efficient and economical manner. In most cases, this objective can best be achieved through international competitive bidding open to qualified contractors or manufacturers from all of the Bank's member countries and Switzerland and Taiwan, China. To foster the development of local capabilities, a degree of preference is accorded to domestic suppliers and, under certain conditions, to domestic contractors. Local competitive bidding, or even construction by the borrower's own forces, may be more economic and efficient in some projects for which the works are too small for international tendering to be appropriate.

Seeing that the agreed-upon procurement rules are observed in practice—a single loan may involve anywhere from a few individual contracts to several hundred—is a time-consuming job and one that the Bank takes very seriously. Sometimes the job is relatively straightforward and routine; on other occasions, major issues arise, as, for example, in a telecommunications or power project when there may be a very close choice among several international suppliers as to which has made the lowest evaluated bid on a multimillion dollar contract. The borrower, not the Bank, is responsible for preparing the specifications and tender documents and evaluating bids. The Bank's role is to make sure that the borrower's work is done properly and the guidelines are observed so that Bank funds may be disbursed for the contract. Any controversy concerning the proposed award is sure to be called promptly to the Bank's attention.

Consultant services in such fields as economics, management, finance, architecture, and engineering also must be contracted for by borrowers. Because the quality of these services is usually of overriding importance and can vary widely among firms, consideration of price, as applied to goods and works, is normally not appropriate, although it may be used in special circumstances. With respect to such contracting by borrowers, the Bank's role—as outlined in recently published guidelines—is to ensure that the firms considered for selection are treated equitably and that the firm selected is able to provide services of appropriate

21

quality. For this work, too, the Bank encourages consideration of qualified firms from the borrowing country—either alone or in joint ventures—as well as firms from other developing countries.

# EVALUATION

While supervision is, in part, a process of learning through experience, it is primarily concerned with that period in the project's life when physical components are being constructed, equipment purchased and installed, and new institutions, programs, and policies put in place. Once these stages are complete, and Bank funds fully disbursed, the level of supervision declines sharply. During the period of active supervision, attention tends to be focused on the problems of the moment. While projects may be subject to ongoing monitoring and evaluation, the need for a more comprehensive approach to evaluating project results has become apparent. In 1970, an evaluation system was established as the final stage in the project cycle.

All Bank-assisted projects are now subject to an *ex post* audit. To ensure its independence and objectivity, this audit is the responsibility of the Operations Evaluation Department (OED), which is entirely separate from the operating staff of the Bank and which reports directly to the Executive Directors. While this system ensures full accountability, it is also designed to mesh closely with, and take advantage of, the supervision activity of the operating staff.

As the final step in supervision, regular projects staff—or the borrower—prepare a completion report on each project at the end of the disbursement period. These reports are, in part, an exercise in self-evaluation—which has not prevented them from being frank and often critical. Each report is reviewed by the OED, which then prepares a separate audit report; both reports are sent to the Executive Directors. Most audits are based on a desk review of all materials pertaining to the project, but, whenever necessary, the audit staff undertakes a field review, sometimes as comprehensive as the original appraisal. Borrowers are asked to comment on the OED audits and are requested to prepare their own completion reports. Furthermore, the Bank encourages borrowers to establish evaluation systems to review all their development investments.

Each audit and completion report re-estimates the economic rate of return on the basis of actual implementation costs and updated information on operating costs and expected benefits. It cannot, however, pass a final judgment on the success or failure of some projects whose economic lives, with their attendant operating costs and benefits, extend well beyond the end of the disbursement period. To meet this need, OED prepares "impact evaluation reports" at least five years after the last disbursement for a small number of carefully selected projects. Borrowers play an active role in this process, too.

In addition, an annual OED report reviews all project audits. Studies are made in greater depth of groups of projects (such as all loans to development finance companies), special problems (such as delays in loan effectiveness), or a sector in a particular country (such as agricultural projects in Indonesia).

The evaluation system is a gold mine of information, supplementing and complementing that provided by the broader stream of project supervision reports. Some of the findings are sobering; many are reassuring. Experience indicates, for example, that the Bank still has much to learn about technologies necessary to bring about sustained increases in yields of small farmers in rainfed areas, most notably in sub-Saharan Africa. Problems of cost overruns and delayed completion have plagued the implementation of a number of projects, particularly in the period following the oil price rises and ensuing worldwide inflation. Many projects change in scope during their implementation. Nevertheless, the most recent* annual review of the OED audits, comprising eighty-seven projects, indicates that over 93 percent of the investments remain worthwhile, and that a number of them had expected economic returns better than those estimated at appraisal.

Particularly gratifying is the indication that the Bank's response to the lessons of experience is generally positive. Mistakes, of which the Bank has had its share, are not often repeated. Subsequent projects build on earlier ones in the same sector. New approaches, policies, and procedures have been adopted to improve project performance: For example, the project brief system is helping to secure government agreement and commitment to project objectives at an earlier stage of project design; rural development projects now integrate the provision of all the services, inputs, and basic infrastructure necessary to bring about a sustained increase in small farmers' yields; lending for projects that are at a more advanced stage of preparation is being introduced to provide more accurate cost estimates and reduce the likelihood of cost overruns and implementation delays.

The lessons of experience are thus being built into the design and preparation of future projects. In other words, the project cycle is working as intended.

*Seventh Annual Review of Project Performance Audit Results. (Washington: World Bank). December 1981.

24

**Borrowers** from the Bank can include a member government, a public agency or corporation, or a private body or corporation with the government's guarantee. IDA credits are made only to governments, to be passed on, if necessary, to the entity responsible for carrying out the project. In this pamphlet, that entity is referred to as the borrower. **Loans** are made by the Bank at an interest rate that is adjusted periodically in relation to the Bank's cost of borrowing. IDA provides **credits** on concessionary terms of 50 years and a minimal service charge. The methods of project work are identical for the two institutions, and in this pamphlet all references to the Bank and to loans apply equally to IDA and to credits.

The **International Finance Corporation** (IFC), which is also an affiliate of the World Bank, has the specific task of furthering economic development by encouraging the growth of productive private enterprise in the developing countries. Its project cycle is different from that of the World Bank and IDA.

**The World Bank**

**Headquarters:**
1818 H Street, N.W.
Washington, D.C. 20433, U.S.A.

Telephone: (202) 477-1234
Telex: WUI 64145 WORLDBANK
　　　　 RCA 248423 WORLDBK
Cable address: INTBAFRAD
　　　　　　　　 WASHINGTONDC

**European Office:**
66, avenue d'Iéna
75116 Paris, France

Telephone: (1) 723-54.21
Telex: 842-620628

**Tokyo Office:**
Kokusai Building
1-1, Marunouchi 3-chome
Chiyoda-ku, Tokyo 100, Japan

Telephone: (03) 214-5001
Telex: 781-26838

**ISBN 0-8213-0022-9**